Reflections
"A JOURNEY TO RETIREMENT"

Ermileta Elliott

authorHOUSE

AuthorHouse™
1663 Liberty Drive
Bloomington, IN 47403
www.authorhouse.com
Phone: 1 (800) 839-8640

Published by AuthorHouse 07/10/2019

ISBN: 978-1-5462-1519-6 (sc)
ISBN: 978-1-5462-1517-2 (e)

Library of Congress Control Number: 2017916928

Print information available on the last page.

Dedication

This anthology of poems is dedicated posthumously to my grandparents of blessed memory. My paternal grandmother, Mrs. Christiana Jeffers, who always impressed upon me the importance of excelling in whatever one does. In addition, I also bestow honor to my maternal grandfather, Mr. Joseph Nathaniel "Dandy" Browne, who loved to include rhymes in conversations. It is also dedicated to those teachers who influenced my love for poetry along with the many who have been taught to enjoy this art in the poet's corner.

Acknowledgements

Over the years, there have been many reflections which gave birth to this production. It is with sincere gratitude to those persons who were always willing to lend a listening ear and expressed great admiration when they heard many of the poems expressed in this anthology.

To my husband, Spencer and our children, Nizron, Nikeeva and Nalkim. In addition, our grandchildren, who always enjoyed practicing and reciting with me whenever an occasion presented itself. To my extended family, cousins, neighbours, friends and numerous well-wishers, I say thank you

Special mention must be made of Mrs. Violet O. Jeffers-Nicholls, Mrs. Lornette Hanley, Ms. Marion Jeffers and Ms. Renita Seabrookes whose assistance with the editing was greatly appreciated.

I would also like to acknowledge the photographer, Mr. Errol Pemberton for the front cover picture and also Mrs. Monica Pemberton for the author's photo on the back cover.

Contents

Patriotism

Religion

Tributes

Education

Limericks

Nature's Voice

Graduation, Harvest, Extravaganza

Secular

Life's Battles

Patriotism

Follow Your Dreams

Believe in yourself!
Learn to say, "Yes, I can!'
For the first step in achieving a dream,
Is to be your own, biggest fan.
Trust your creativity
To find a way to pull through.
Follow your instincts,
Instead of the old tried and true.
Nothing worthwhile comes easily!
Sometimes it's going to be tough,
But keep on the positive side of the road.
Don't try to carry it all at once
For that is too heavy a load.
Don't be too proud to listen
For wisdom has saved many dreams.
When you swim in those currents that will get you upstream
You're meant to achieve what your heart tells you inside.
Listen to that inner voice ....
It will always be your guide.

Our Duty to our Nation

To do our duty every man,
Is the cry of citizens in this fair land.
We have to preserve our independence
By working hard and being a people with confidence.

Children too have to learn in school,
There is no reason to play the fool.
With commitment and dedication,
We can obtain valuable education.

Adults too have to play their part,
By setting examples for our youth from the start.
There should be no idling on the job each day,
Hard work should be the hallmark of our people today.

At work, employees should act professionally,
Not only when the boss is around and then pretend to be busy.
Presence or absence of the boss, one is paid to do the job.
Every minute that is wasted, our economy goes one step backward.

For these years, we give thanks to the Almighty,
Our country is making progress surely.
Airport and seaport, country and town,
Even rebuilding the old treasury, which was burnt down.

Independence Anniversary

Independence anniversary is a joyful occasion,
When our country celebrates.
Our nation became independent in 1983!
So welcome to our celebration
For our beautiful little nation.

They Toiled and Toiled

Combermere School stands on an estate
Where our forefathers toiled.
They had to sweat in the heat of the midday sun,
And when the master spoke, they had to run.
Their blood was shed, this was no fun
When they toiled, and toiled, and toiled.

It was real hard work, from dawn until dusk,
From Monday to Saturday, this was a must.
Yet they had an aim to make life better,
As they worked on small plots to grow peas, corn and pepper.
They had a vision for their children's future,
As they toiled, and toiled, and toiled.

Today, as we reminisce after many years
Progress has been made but we have further to go.
Every child has access to education,
We will guard this treasure with care and caution.
And never forget our forefathers contribution to our nation,
When they toiled, and toiled, and toiled.

The Caribbean

The Caribbean is a place we love so dear,
Let us treasure what we have right here
And for each other care.
The social ills, let's drive them out
While keeping illegal drugs from our shores.
Even if we are angry,
Let us exhibit self-control to discuss and settle the problem amicably.

The Meaning of Independence

I - I must now decide to learn in school,
   Attend regularly, and not play the fool.

N - Never to look back but forward always,
   Ever strive to improve in the coming days.

D – Diligent at home, at school, in sports,
   Forever strive to achieve an excellent report.

E - Eager to help both old and young -
   The feeble, the disabled, the blind and the dumb.

P – Peer pressure will not force me to do wrong
   Because I will stand for what is right in the throng.

E – Energetic and full of life
   Avoiding trouble and keeping away from strife.

N – Noble and nimble for our country I'll be,
   As only the best is good enough in our country.

D – Dedicated toward upholding human rights -
   Avoid abusing, swearing and also fights.

E – Striving to get rid of our social ills
   Like bullying, terrorism and cleaning up oil spills.

N – Numerically, I'll be on the ball,
   An expert mathematician will be my call.

C – Courageously committed to family and friends,
   Continually believing in them to achieve favourable ends.

E – Enforcing always the golden rule,
   Controlling anger and remaining cool.

This is our solemn message to you!
Join our bandwagon, it is the Independence crew.

Independence 25 Elocution Victory

(Dedicated to Nijaunte David, Quetta Daniel and Shadecia Allen)

Independence 25 in Nevis had an Elocution Competition.
When all primary schools participated in the action.
This was a moment in our history,
When each school would participate in three categories

VOJN[1] Primary had Nijaunte David, Quetta Daniel and Shadecia Allen.
The objective was for each contestant to win.
Parents rallied around the students' cause,
It was real hard work preparing them without a pause.

Finally, came the day of the competition.
The old cinema building was the venue for the action.
Teachers encouraged all three not to relent,
As a contingent of supporters would surely be present.

Nijaunte David, contestant number nine, stepped on to the podium and had no fear.
Her confidence level was high and her distinct expressions were clear.
When she finished there was such a tremendous applause,
A stunning smile beamed across Nijaunte's face when she paused.

---

[1] Violet O. Jeffers-Nicholls Primary School

Representing the middle school in Grade Four was Quetta;
Her enunciation was perfect to the very last letter.
The approval for this contestant was even greater,
Her performance made her the champion later.

Finally, it was Shadecia's turn in Grade Six.
It was hoped she would give the other contestants licks.
Forward she moved on that concrete stage,
And conveyed her message having the audience fully engaged.

Unofficial judging now followed as to who would win.
The excited audience gazed at the trophies in waiting.
It was perfect silence when the official judges came forward and
spoke;
VOJN won in each segment and this was no joke!

For all these were electrifying, exhilarating moments,
The triple blast had been completed by our articulate students!

Religion

The Marks of a Healthy Church

A healthy church is a learning church,
Which should grow in knowledge and grace.
There must be listening and prayer each day,
Praising together in every place.

A healthy church is a growing church,
Telling of the love of God.
Our attitudes and actions should send the message
That we are followers exemplary of Christ.

A healthy church is an inclusive church,
Willing to give each person a chance.
To display one talent in and away from the church,
Whether to read, heal, teach or dance.

A healthy church is a relevant church
Catering to the needs of people.
Addressing issues, sharing ideas and solutions
In honest discussions which will glorify God.

Thank God for our Fathers

We thank God for our fathers,
The love and care they share.
For providing daily bread
And comfort, in times of despair.

We owe a debt of gratitude
For support they give.
Help us always to be thankful Lord,
For fathers, as long as they live.

Our Fathers here at Combermere
Have been a blessing Lord.
In tasks they do both great and small
Fathers, we thank you one and all.

Who Do You Say That I Am?

Between the Gentiles and the Jews,
The question by Jesus was asked,
"Who do you say that I am?
Tell me, what are your views?"

Confusing poor Herod, who said this could be John,
Or maybe even Elias.
Yes, Herod recognized that this man was different
But yet did not recognize the Messiah.

As per usual, Peter, the man who would speak,
Rebuked Jesus when He spoke of His death.
"Get thee behind me, Satan," Jesus declared,
"You have no interest the things of God."

Even today, questions are still being asked,
"Who do you say that I am?"
His teachings definitely declared,
"I am Jesus Christ, the Son of God."

Dust Your Feet Off

On a visit to Jane's garden,
I saw roses in full bloom.
Then I thought about the city
Where there is neither death nor doom.

So, dust your feet off,
Lift your chin up,
Square your shoulders and just look up.

The cross is a symbol of hope that we see
And everlasting life for eternity.
Let's rise up and take what is offered to all,
Salvation, so full, so rich and free.

Carry the sword of the spirit in your hand
Over every 'nook and cranny' in this land.
On your head put the helmet of salvation,
And in your mind some commitment and dedication.

Life may seem dreary and sometimes tough,
The road may get lonely and very rough;
This is the time when courage will show,
And out of these challenges, you will certainly grow.

Chosen For Such A Time

Christ enables us to fulfil our calling
Having been liberated from many things;
The joy of forgiveness Christ offers to us,
The mind, love, attitude and also His purpose.

When an opportunity arises, be ready to serve,
Let others know our redemption has been paid;
We must have loving and forgiving hearts
To welcome all into the fold of God.

While there is life, there is hope,
To reach the throne of grace;
Being in Christ has liberty, strength and power
Chosen for such a time as this hour.

The Brand

(Inspired by a sermon from Rev. Dennis Baptiste)

God wants us to market His brand
And display a product that speaks of His way.
Where He is in charge of our lives
As we live for Him day by day.

This brand was paid for by the blood of Jesus
Over two thousand years ago.
We must market our Lord from the inside out,
In our homes, our schools, and at work.

This brand has withstood the test of time,
When he healed the sick and made the lame walk.
At the wedding in Cana, he turned water into wine
And he made the dumb talk, says Mark Chapter nine.

The brand says don't fear those who can kill the body
But fear Him who can destroy body and soul in hell.
This Brand must be on the streets of the world
So invite Him in our hearts and homes to dwell.

When this brand changes us from the inside out,
It will be an experience one has to talk about.
The brand is free, so in God we'll put our trust
We have to get it brethren, that is a must!

The brand is about prayer and having peace in the heart,
It can prevent marriages from falling apart.
This brand wants the Church to change the world,
And save hearts that over years have grown cold.

This brand will help us to love your enemies,
And for truth always take a stand.
We will never feel ashamed of the Word of God;
For God Almighty's sake, let us market the brand!

Deliverance

Sin oppresses, depresses, possesses,
And becomes a loophole for Satan's entry.
Evil weakens marriage and also the family,
So we must identify and eradicate it quickly.

Man's effort can never treat his sinful condition;
It's a freedom that must be obtained by the Saviour's redemption.
Where there is lack of strength, vision or grace,
Deliverance is needed at the Saviour's place.

Remember, Jesus met the woman at the well,
When he passed through Samaria where this woman dwelt.
Jesus said, "Your condition is not your conclusion
Get up and get rid of your confusion."

We must come into contact with Jesus,
For to Him our lives are so very precious.
Come, see a man who told me all that I did,
There is now a difference that cannot be hid.

(Poem inspired by Sermon from Rev. Benilda Manswell-Daniel 19-05-16)

A Man of Virtue

A man of virtue, a man of grace,
Your love for all will never be erased.
That calm personality was loved so much,
Your principles and humility just had fine touch.
Standing for truth and righteousness,
Speaking firmly, with little aggressiveness.
Exemplary for big and small,
Encouraging members to answer God's call.

Upon your toes you used to go,
With fingers pointing while the Word was preached, we know.
Years of love was displayed by our preacher,
With dedication and commitment, you were a teacher.
Thanks for the time you spent in your second home,
Continue spreading God's Word, as we are only here on loan.
You'll always remain in our thoughts here,
Memories will linger for many years.

To Count the Many Blessings

To count the many blessings,
We have received each day.
Would take us oh so many years,
Those counts might just erase.

Just think about the food we eat,
The air we breathe so clean.
The beauty of the plants,
And grass that grow so green.

Many thousand things just come to mind
As we go on our way.
We may not be rich by the world's standard
But spiritually, we are blessed.

So as we sojourn along life's way,
Just whisper a thankful prayer.
For people, blessings, great and small
In God's sight we will stand tall.

The Request, The Report, The Return

The prodigal son he made a request,
It seemed as though he meant to put his dad to a test.
Now Dad, I'd like to get all of my own,
I'll go into a far country to have some seeds sown.
Father thought in his mind, but didn't say no,
The inexperienced young lad got ready to go.

He left with such happiness there was no way to tell
That one day his life would reach near the gates of hell.
Friends all around him with money to spend,
Never thought that one day, on swine food he would depend.
With money now finished, all his friends disappeared.
His report now suggested that nobody cared.

Sitting in a pig sty, he envied the pigs,
For into coconut husks, he began to dig.
He thought to himself, "Man, this shouldn't be me.
Dad has food in abundance I'm going home to see."
The decision was made slowly but with some wisdom.
He returned straight home to his father's kingdom.

While the young man was still a long distance away,
Dad looked and shouted, "I glimpse my son coming this way!"
The son inched home and had sincere apology.
"Boy look," said Dad, "You are the one I'm so pleased to see,
Servants, bring now the fattest calf from over in the pasture,
Let's celebrate and have a party in splendour!"

Forgiven, the son could hardly believe
That such a rapturous welcome he would receive.
His bruised, tired feet now had new shoes on,
His robe and ring were the best in the land.
"Come, my dear son, I'm so glad you are here,
I certainly missed you and I honestly care."

What great love this father had for his son!
Imagine God's eternal love for everyone.
The prostitutes, liars, thieves and drug addicts,
The drunkards, the terrorists and the boastful with bad habits.
His encompassing love showers down on us all,
We just have to repent and answer his call.

Prayer

Prayer
Prayer changes things
When it is sincere;
It also directs people how to care.

Wisdom
A prayer for wisdom
Is important each day,
Asking for guidance along the way.

Patience
A prayer to have patience
To work with discontented colleagues
Who sometimes seem beseiged.

Admit
A prayer to admit
When a mistake is made,
And not to begin a useless tirade.

Forgiveness

A prayer of forgiveness
When we feel others have done wrong,
This will help to make us strong.

Tributes

A Tribute to Pastor Eversley Pemberton

A man of dignity, courage and humility!
Walked daily among us so peaceful and lowly;
As Pastor and Overseer he showed commitment and dedication,
His purpose was to see people receive salvation.

The New Testament Church of God in Fountain was his very first mission,
That must have been a serious decision.
The harvest was ripe but the reapers were few,
He put his hand to the plough, as there was much work to do.

Members in Charlestown you also served well,
You encouraged people to stay out of hell.
Pastor Eversley Pemberton, you've stood the test
Giving forty years of service to God, we salute you for doing your best!

Tribute to Donna Browne

The Nevis Teachers' Union is quite pleased tonight
To honour one of its long standing members with immeasurable delight.
On the Executive, she has served in various capacities,
Starting in 1989 as Assistant General Secretary.

In any activity that Donna Browne had to participate,
Things had to be done properly or she would articulate.
At times, some of the things that she would daresay
Would make one wonder if she went 'off course' a little that day.

Donna Browne loved the Nevis Teachers' Union dearly.
And when teachers did not play their part her frustration was shown quite clearly.
At the inauguration when Teachers turned up at the well decorated community center,
Donna was elated and exclaimed, "I could not have felt better".

The NTU has been represented overseas by Donna on many occasions,
From Bahamas in the North to Trinidad in the south at CUT functions
She managed the athletic team which awarded NTU, great attention!
Just imagine one of our athletes was Victor Lodorum.

Her infectious laughter will always echo in our ears
And she could also make you laugh until you're brought to tears.
When it came to Union business dealing with money,
Donna ensured that things were done in order and with scrutiny.

This lady of whom I speak is always immaculately dressed,
And her neat handwriting is hard to beat in any contest.
For Donna, only the best was sufficient,
For the Nevis Teachers' Union she was certainly very efficient.

Donna, the Nevis Teachers' Union expresses its gratitude to you.
Though you may blush, it's for all that you have done and will continue to do.
Thanks, for a job well done from the very start
From 1989 t0 2014, you have played an outstanding part.

D   Dedicated and dynamic
O   Observant
N   Never yielding
N   Naturally nice
A   Authentic

Reverend Baptiste

Like Elisha you took up the Methodist mantle in Nevis some years ago,
And from then on the seeds of righteousness you endeavoured to sow.
With prayer and supplication we were encouraged to stand in the gap
For our brethren, on life's journey, when they experienced hard knocks.

You preached your sermons with passion, and yes, there was much perspiration,
And sometimes when you hit the nail on the head, you'd just laugh.
Ha! Ha! Amen! You're with Me?
That "Yes Mon" would not be forgotten by any congregation.
Whether it was Bible Study, funeral, morning worship, or in a cordial conversation.

Some would remember when you exhorted about marketing God's Brand,
As criminal activities spiralled in the streets of our land.
You opined, "The Brand is about prayer and having peace in the heart,
We must market the Brand at work, in school, but in our homes to start."

This Brand will help you to love your enemies,
And for truth and righteousness always take a stand.
We must never feel ashamed of the Word of God.
"Good God, Almighty", your voice thundered, "Let us market The Brand!"

Don't think for one moment you'll only be missed by Methodists,
Brother you've had resounding spiritual impact on many more in Nevis.
The conscientious effort you made to reach out to all,
To share spiritual guidance which is your call.

The fruits of your labour may only sometimes be seen,
But we'll continue in the vineyard preparing for our soon coming
King.
Preparation will continue to help families in the future,
Plus the interest in our youth, their young minds to nurture.

It is with grace, we salute your dear wife,
Being the spouse of a pastor can sometimes be a challenging life.
Thanks to you and the children for supporting him,
He certainly would have liked each soul in our island for Jesus to win.

Rev. Baptiste, as you return to the land of your birth,
May God continue to protect, to guide and lead you in his work.
Combermere is simply placing on record
Our appreciation for what you have done for our Lord.

Bernadine's Retirement

(With acknowledgements to Bevelyn Jones and Althea Jones)

No need for an explanation
Because from her creation
She was born a pretty baby,
Whom everyone called Cutie.

Her schooling began at the great Comberemere All Age School in Nevis,
Where she was taught by quality teachers.
One classmate recalls Bernadine was never absent whether it was sunshine or rain,
She loved school and would never complain.

After passing the College of Preceptors exam, called C.P.
She then continued her education at the Charlestown Secondary.
Following her academic achievement, she chose the teaching profession.
Tonight, after thirty eight years, she is being given a stalwart's recognition.

Bernadine was a founding member of the New Testament Church of God, Fountain,
Where she assisted the youth in overcoming hurdles and mountains.
She is a dedicated and committed Christian,
Looking forward to living with Jesus in that heavenly mansion.

In 1978, she started working at the Basseterre Girls School and later went on to Beach Allen,
There she had an educational impact on the lives of thousands.
Children couldn't form the fool in Miss Hanley's class, not even in their dreams,
As business and discipline reigned supreme.

College days from 1982 – 1984 were filled with hard work and fun,
With colleagues who sometimes got frustrated and tried to run.
Who would ever forget Tanty Pearl sporting?
Or the girls lighting the candles when we were graduating?

Bernadine, on your retirement, we wish you all the best!
By God you have been favoured, you are so very blessed.
Congratulations! May your life continue to be an inspiration.
Thank you girl, you have served the teaching profession with distinction.

Happy Retirement to you Bernadine,
Now you are being honoured as our Teaching Queen!
Thirty eight years of service now our heroine,
HAPPY RETIREMENT TO YOU BERNADINE!

Inspiration, Vision, Transformation

Inspired by a vision
Reverend Gumbs started on a mission
To erect a new Methodist Church in Fountain
Close to Nevis' pristine mountain.

Dissatisfied with the condition of the older building
That was just not to his taste and liking--
Unsuitable to worship God, our Father
So seeds he started to sow for others to garner.

Our local people along with an overseas team
Worked together for the common good.
Many persons hands were bruised,
As they pounded stones to erect the new structure.

The stone works were done mainly by Oral and Fanso
Those boys truly sweat as they were on the go.
A contractor came in when the structure reached beam height,
Now members had to deal with the financial plight.

For countless years God has been good to our people
Amidst many problems and natural disasters.
Investing in missions, we must seek to save souls
That should be our most important goal.

Today, the problems are greater, we know,
Our culture has changed from a few years ago.
Social graces seemed to have gone down the drain,
Bullets from guns are falling on us like rain.

The Church in general has much work to do,
To help save lost souls from destruction, that's true!
Churches get lots of blame from high and low
But when disaster strikes – check one of the first places people go!

Fountain has had all these and more,
Let's fight the good fight and press for the beautiful shore.
Now growing in strength, the test has now only begun
We're investing in souls and with that mission we must run.

It took inspiration to bring about a vision for transformation.

Forty Years of Dedicated Service

"I've had an enjoyable nursing career," smiled
Nurse Adriene Ward-Stanley
With cheeks glowing all the while.
If I had to do it all over again,
In that same field I'd surely train.

On September 9, 1974 this star from Mt. Lily stepped forth,
Into the field of nursing she went walking honourably through the
ranks.
From Student Nurse to Staff Nurse wearing a red belt,
To the blue belt as Sister and then the brown belt as Nurse Manager.

Our nurse did not dwell on her laurels.
There are numerous stories which she can tell.
She eventually became assistant matron
And was given excellent commendation.

Forty years of dedicated service and commitment,
Whether morning, evening or night shift.
Our people are proud of your unwavering contribution
To our twin island Federation.

Oh, the challenges were many as she assisted patients,
But the successes were even more with her serene personality.
As midwife she delivered many babies on the Maternity ward,
Many little ones, she served on the Pediatric Ward

Thank you for forty years of health care you gave.
Congratulations, no wealth along the way you craved!
Thank God, you retired with hardly get a cold,
May your cup be always filled with blessings manifold.

Sister Audriene Ward-Stanley, today, Combermere salutes you for your years of hard work

Rev. Careen Whyte-Richardson

Rev. Careen came to Nevis some years ago,
To encourage Christ's flock and ensure members grow.
At one of our Methodist churches she was stationed
To make her mark spiritually on this little nation.

That high pitched voice used to command rapt attention,
As members were led in prayer and she expounded in sermons.
On television some referred to her as the dancing preacher
In the pulpit she educated like a master teacher.

She came to this land with the surname Whyte,
But then her eyes were attracted to a beacon bright.
It was the Anguillan she decided to wed.
Now he is the husband with whom she shares daily bread.

Brother, for your service in Nevis there is much appreciation.
We will always remember your quiet disposition.
Please keep the flames burning with your devoted heart-warming,
And I believe our dear lady would keep singing and dancing.

Now, as you prepare to leave
Many blessings from us you now receive.
Our country extends heartfelt gratitude to you
For what you have both done, and for being faithful and true.

Rev. Careen

Ready to serve with **R**ighteousness
Energized with daring **E**xploits
Vivacious and full of **V**igour

Caring lady with great **C**oncern
Amicable while **A**dmonishing
Relentless in telling about Christ's **R**esurrection
Eager to enhance and **E**ncourage
Entertaining and **E**difying
Never to forget **N**evis

Ernestine Alberta France

May 19 in 1926, a beautiful baby girl in Scarborough was born.
She brought such joy to her mother on that Wednesday morn.
Great things God has done and Ernestine is giving Him the glory
As she is now celebrating and praising Him now that she's ninety.

She was christened with the names Ernestine Alberta,
And soon she was walking around as a toddler.
Her Mother, Iva Wilkes, cared for her until she was seven,
Then died shortly after, Ernestine hopes to meet her in heaven.

Having this tragedy so early in life
She was raised by her dad, Ebenezer and Olga his wife.
These were days of fun with her siblings in Mt. Lily,
Where they had to look after pigs, sheep and cattle, which were
plenty.

Growing into adulthood she started her own family
Having nine children, the eldest being Carlyle known as Pepsi.
Shirley, Fernella, Sheila, Sylvester, Jennifer, Jacqueline, Laurel and
Dinsey would follow.
Life was not easy but Ernestine was a determined and diligent worker.

Farming at Nisbett's and Camps provided the family with daily bread;
Her breakfast menu included cow's milk, fried dumplings and
potatoes and her famous corn porridge,
Johnny cakes and eggs were the specialities for lunch
With a big jar of lemonade and some fruits for everybody to crunch.

Education for Ernestine's children was a priority.
Good manners and self-respect and humility
Combermere School could tell many tales
When you didn't do your domestic chores then across she would sail.

Ernestine was one of Camps Village sugar cake makers.
She sold frozen joy and was also a baker.
Ernestine believed in great entertainment
So she took the children to Peas Patch for Saturday night merriment.

She gave care to some elderly people in her community;
Some would remember Markie Dorcas, Dummy James and Cattie.
Neighbourhood children like Lisa and Kinky,
And many more as her extended family.

Her children and grandchildren had no choice when it came to
worshipping God
She taught them to serve Him as Saviour and Lord.
Forget all excuses when it came to going to church
She set them the example, and in front of them would march.

Now residing in the United States with daughter, from 1992
Her children say she loves to dress with matching hat and shoes.
She loves game shows when the time is right,
As they give her much relaxation and delight.

Ernestine is still in good health and moving around.
She is counting her blessings from a mind that is sound.
Today, we salute our ninety year old Taurean Queen
Our gratitude to you for the mother you have been.

(Chorale) CHILDREN, GRAND CHILDREN AND GREAT
GRANDCHILDREN

Ma, Oh Ma, you are simply the best
Today, you are our honoured guest
Because of you our lives have been blessed.
Ma, oh Ma, you are simply the best!

Tribute to a St. Lucian Jockey

On to the teaching race track stepped a St. Lucian racehorse,
Eager to put on her show.
On its back it carried a slim young jockey,
Rearing and ready to go.

The year was 1971.
The track was in Bobanneau.
The jockey was Virginia;
With Pegasus' wings this 'greenhand' flew.

She carefully observed each situation,
And with help she had much preparation.
In her mind was intrinsic motivation,
And into teaching put her dedication.

The Trained Teacher's Certificate she gained on home ground
Gathered speed with the Bachelor's on her second round.
The Masters in Human Resource Management was ahead
Following by an Executive Diploma for which she jumped ahead.

Teaching she loved and with much articulation,
Improved the morale of teachers with love and devotion.
Respected, indomitable is the jockey on her horse.
Now, for the Status of Women, she is fighting the cause.

Bobanneau choraled, "This is our most outstanding woman!"
And for long service, the Teachers' Union placed her on the Awards bandwagon,
Such a talented lady St. Lucia observed,
For her a national award was now reserved.

Tribute to Poets in the Square

Oh yeh, Oh yeh, all who hear tell who no hear,
This is another edition of POETS IN THE SQUARE.
It was a Nevisian's unique idea
To encourage our poets, their talents to share.
So today again please just lend an ear
To Nevisian Poets in the Square!

During the Culture Season people visit from the West and the East
From midday to one o'clock to enjoy the listening feast.
Remember Nevis has a creative University,
Which was created by your grandpa and my granny.
So today again please just lend an ear,
To Nevisian Poets in the Square!

Our seniors have given full support
To something they inherited and know about.
Check out how themselves they well express,
We salute them now because they are the best.
So again today, please lend an ear
To Nevisian Poets in the Square.

Sometimes guest poets from St. Kitts and Antigua
Come to join in the poetry fiesta.
Some are passionate activists
Whose opinion is that crimes should not be lightly dismissed.
So again today please lend an ear
To our many Poets in the Square.

Poetry is an art form which Caribbean people enjoy,
As one expresses with rhythms, tone, emotions and other ploys.
To all our poets and our audiences who joined the fun,
We say a big thank you to everyone.
So until next year try and compose with a special ear
For Culturama's, "Nevisian Poets in the Square."

Nevis Teachers' Union

(Dedicated to teachers in Nevis)

A Union! A Union! Some teachers cried,
We'll unite as one for the fraternity's pride.
Many years ago we made a start
With the first President James Neale, who had a brave heart.

The going was slow, the road was rough,
Convincing teachers about their rights was tough.
Unionizing seemingly had a negative connotation.
'Twas mainly the primary school teachers who joined the organisation.

The second president was Laurence Richards,
With Althea Jones being the third.
Adina Taylor was fourth and Wakely Daniel was fifth.
Ermileta Elliott was sixth, and Ornette Webbe seventh.

The first elected General Secretary was Marcella Jones.
Her assistant being Donna Browne.
They recorded the Nevis Teachers' Union minutes;
Month after month, without a frown.

NTU[2], assisted by CUT[3] and CTF[4]
Has certainly made steady progress
Attending conferences, workshops and seminars,
From Bermuda down to Guyana.

---

[2] Nevis Teachers' Union
[3] Caribbean Union of Teachers
[4] Canadian Teachers Federation

In Zimbabwe, Olvis Dyer attended the first World Congress;
Althea Jones' trip to Thailand was also a success.
Executive members have benefited from training at workshops,
And have also been exposed to the John Thompson Fellowship.

Nevis Teachers' Union has persevered over the years,
Upholding the hands of teachers. Yes it cares!
The struggle is on, some days we had fun,
There were years of hard labour but many victories we have won.

Education

Teachers

Teachers have a repertoire of information we know
As they nurture the children with seeds that they sow.
Some show love and care.
Some are firm and fair.
Some display little concern whether children learn or know.

Teachers are the pillars of this nation
Who should treasure each child as a unique creation.
Teachers should show commitment,
Helping attitudes with positive development,
Thus, shaping lives with motivation and encouragement.

Brenda's Pudding

When a group of teachers planned to visit Canada,
Each member decided to start a fund raiser.
One invested in potato pudding,
That was her way of money making.

The marketing strategy went very well
As Friday after Friday her pudding did sell;
Each week the demand got greater and greater,
This gave birth to the idea to continue sales later.

Customers expressed great satisfaction,
Their reviews commanded national attention.
That was the invention of the Brenda's brand,
The best potato pudding in this island.

Always Be Prepared

What I learned at my colleague's table is, "Always be prepared,"
For anything that can go wrong will certainly go wrong.
It happens when important things are due to start on time,
And suddenly, out of the blue, a problem will emerge.

Imagine, an activity at nine thirty was due to start.
At ten fifteen, participants and officers stood at the gate in a public
path.
The phones were ringing left and right and in and out of town,
Still no one could track down the keys or get access to the grounds.

One officer, when contacted, said instructions had been given to the
staff,
But those members probably didn't understand or possibly had on
their earphone masks.
Embarrassment simply filled the entire tent;
Passersby wondered if there had been a terrible accident.

Next, one high ranking officer came with one employee in tow,
Though an explanation was given, it was obvious this was a mighty
blow.
The damage had been done. There was humiliation and heads were
down;
Even a blind man realized that the captain was not in this ship's bow.

So whenever events are being planned, always be prepared,
'Cause what I gained at my colleague's table, my imagination would
not have dared.

Those Who Can Read

Those who can read sometimes don't read carefully,
Especially when fine prints on a document they see.
Like those that are on an insurance document
Or the passenger ticket that has the vitally important content.

Those who enter the exit and not the entrance
And don't check the amount on the credit card balance.
At ten o'clock they see bus should leave the departure gate
And arrive at ten fifteen seemingly expecting it to wait.

An organizer should hint the importance of time management
And so refrain from the key note speaker not being compliant
Those who see the notes and refuse to study
And then get jealous of a successful buddy.

It is hard to believe that those who can read
Sometimes fail to do so carefully.

I Try And I Try

Some of my classmates find reading so easy
But somehow this skill makes me uneasy.
I try and I try and it's so hard to tell
Why I just can't read or spell very well.

Words are difficult to pronounce and remember.
Whether it's 'was' or 'saw', my mind is in a blunder.
My teacher gets impatient and angry
And poor me, oh dear, am in a quandary.

Parents can't understand how I sometimes read so fluently
Yet to spell and write, these two puzzle me sorely.
The shackles of comprehension are tying me down
When I don't understand, I feel like the class clown.

Matching letter and sound is a continuous bother
I've just got to repeat them over and over.
Teacher tries to help and sometimes get frustrated.
I now feel like a lost lamb abdicated.

My day of redemption has finally come
A Reading Specialist is now at the Department of Education
Travelling around from school to school
Motivating students and helping them to achieve as a rule.

With patience we are encouraged, "Try and try again
You can do it my child, this will not be in vain."
Excitement can be heard in that quiet voice
To learn to read, I must, there is no other choice.

Birthday Greetings Mother, Dear

So many times I've wished that you were here.
Or, perhaps that I was there.
And then each other's love we would share,
"Birthday greetings, Mother Dear!"

But since you are so far away
And I can't feel your embrace today.
I'd just like to express it this simple way
"Enjoy your birthday, Mother, I pray."

You wouldn't know the many sighs,
I've often thought and wondered why
I've never shared this special day with you.
And this comes from a heart sincere and true.

However, your eldest wishes you good cheer.
"A blessed Birthday, Mother Dear!"

$\mathcal{P}apa$

My tall and stately Papa
Was tall and generous.
He saved some snacks for us each day
Especially cheetos.

Papa was a man of virtue,
Hardworking, he was, too.
A loving, caring family man,
Revered by the entire Jones clan.

He left us all so suddenly!
We just don't understand.
But pleasant memories will live on,
Because we believe he's gone to a better land.

Daddy Cares

I looked into my Daddy's eyes,
They had a puzzled look.
It seemed as though he simply stared
Into the world, with all its cares.
Then gently Daddy lifted me and said,
"Son, your Daddy cares."

Again his solemn, gazing stare,
Just frowned and looked away.
It seemed he saw a distant light,
When suddenly, his face shone bright.
Tapping on my shoulders he said,
"Son, your Daddy cares."

It Depends on Who is Sitting in The Chair

When things happen in life and we assess situations,
We sit and configure each day.
We ask ourselves questions
And try to discover if this really was the right way.
One little incident can cause a big stir,
But it depends on who is sitting in the chair.

When changes come in our lives
Do we really adjust?
Or get bitter and sit by and frown?
Can we honestly look the next man in the eyes
And give support, even if he's the bad guy?
One little incident can cause a big stir
It depends on who's sitting in the chair.

When things go wrong and we're really displeased
What is our response day by day?
Do we loiter and lament or play the blame game
Or evaluate issues objectively?
One little incident can cause a great stir,
It depends on who is sitting in the chair.

Reflections

Years ago, when things were tough,
Mt. Lily and Fountain people had life rough.
But these folks had grit and determination,
To see their children succeed with hard work and dedication.

Cooking on three stones was the order of the day,
Then the coal pot was there in case rain came they say.
An overnight firewood was saved to light the fire next morning,
But if rain came that night, there would be problems to get the fire going.

Fountain children didn't go home from school for lunch,
So they ate johnny cakes and sardines with lemonade as the punch.
Many children sat under the flambouyant tree
Down by "Finey Ram Nisbett Restaurant," you see.

Social graces were there in abundance
"Good morning, please and thank you" all walked in accordance.
Don't believe that because some parents disagreed
That, as a child you could exhibit discourtesy on the streets.

At Mount Pleasant, Round Hill, Conu Ghaut and Hog Valley.
Our people never went to Charlestown to buy fruits and vegetables,
Nutritious home grown food used to supply each table.
This is a fact, it is not a fable.

Talent galore was in Mt. Lily and Fountain,
The best player of the trumpet was Braygin.
The village had a professional seamstress
Marsh and Hilda were the physiotherapists.

The special tonic drink in these villages was sarsaparilla
Olga, Emile, Papa George, Finey, Elsie and Ernest were the makers,
From all over Nevis people came to buy this "underground current"
drink,
It was said to possess aphrodisiac qualities that would make you wink.

Brother Nolan was driving from Newcastle to Mt. Lily one day,
Met a lady and gave her a lift, so people say.
Nolan felt he had speed going around a bend,
He said, "Hold your hat girl, Maude, a gon touch ten".

Easter Saturday morning a vendor was going to St. Kitts;
She wanted to travel on the sailboat, Princess.
Vendor said, Lord Mr. Maney, speed up de truck so I can catch de
boat to go down.
Hear Maney's reply, "I'm not going to Basseterre, I'm going to
Charlestown."

Nicknames in the villages are not very new,
Like Marma, Nonsense, Badword, Scraps, Bloke and Labou.
Crab Juice, Trash, Dandy, Scarta, Skull and Tobi
Monkey, Spoon, Knife, Shine, Jarty, Mackerel and Red Mamee.

How can anybody forget Book-u-Look?
And de flying Dow from de Cock family?
Quibus, Drake, Squeeze-E-Eye and Money Glut,
Megs, Mandol, Labour, King Caw and Big Knot?

Those good old days Fountain and Mt. Lily people will always remember,
With thoughts of 'stewing down' the home grown fowl in December.
We thank our forefathers for their dedication,
True love, and hearts, which had great aspirations.

The Master Chef

Turning local produce into refined dishes
Was the advertisement heard on the air.
The venue was the Franklyn Browne Community Center
Where applicants were invited to enter
The facilitator was St. James Chef, Mr. Sylvester Wallace.

Eager to learn thirty students turned up
Waiting to fill their culinary cups
Into four groups the class was divided
With two males who were avid.

Group Number One had Millicent as their leader
They always were early because they were huge consumers.
Group number two had Earlene in command
Boy you could hear her voice booming and directing the clan

Petite Cindy led group three quietly
With comedian Christine acting as deputy
Carol was in charge of Group Number Four
Which was nearly always last to go through the door.

We learned and had fun for three months every Wednesday
With Sylvester's culinary skills educating all the way.

Camps

Combermere School was a central point in Camps
Where children received their formal education.
From the surrounding villages came all the stories
Well, those were the good old days of glory.

Teacher Lorraine Henry-Browne always had a bakery
And to compete with that shop nearby was De Christy.
Fudge came from Lady Ward, and you couldn't make a mistake
Like when we visited Mrs. Norfie's's shop and 'tief' her sugar cakes.

Now people know a male sheep is called a ram
But Camps had Finey and Simeon Ram.
There was also a lady called Ping-Pang
And "Who You" would sing her special song.

Garnet was the village pre-school teacher
Isabella was a musical leader
Another lady said you "Tap Too Long"
And Jim Barker had three eyes – His sight was too strong.

James Daniel was a head teacher, who had eyes that were sharp,
This man used to patrol Combermere School like a hawk.
Before him were "Steplight" Richie and Shatum Edwards
After them came Frank Morton and Melford Ward.

Camps Village had many more characters,
That could be written in many chapters.
We thank these humble people, who had great ambition,
Who ensured that our youth made the right decisions.

Love

Long time ago when people fell in love,
Some people say they use to behave like ground doves.
So when Maria and Don became intimate friends
Don spoke to her father who gave his consent.

In the days of Jerry Ko Ka, it is said lots of things used to go on,
When men's infidelity seemed to be the order of the day.
The good ladies used to keep real cool,
While their spouses went out to form the fool.

Well, there was a couple named Weasy and Ging
Them people were in love like sugar and thing.
But after dem married for many years,
Satan decided he wanted to step up dem stairs.

Weasy Ging decided to friend she best friend's husband
Weasy couldn't believe such a thing could happen.
Who you think Ging live wid now?
Me nar go no further, work out dat somehow.

Pan Dem Phone

(In Nevisian Dialect - Drumology)

Nowadays, wherever you go,
No matter what you do,
People simply always pan dem phone.

You go in a de school,
Teachers pan dem phone.
Politicians in de House
And dem pan dem phone.
Lard wherever you day,
No matter what you say,
People simply always pan dem phone.

De parson a preach,
Members pan dem phone.
Lawyers can't reach clients
Cause dem pan dem phone.
People nar check out de traffic,
Crossing de road with a racket
Carrying a real heavy packet,
And dem pan dem phone.

Something happen in de school
Students pan dem phone.
Parents abusing de Principal
Pan dem phone.
Nar wait to find out how story go,
Whether it is true or it is not so;

Some even want to give a blow,
Even when dem pan dem phone.

You day pan de ferry
People pan dem phone
Home they listening to de TV
Yet dem pan dem phone.
Even in dem exam
Students cause distraction,
Mek dem get expulsion
'Cause dem pan phone

You traveling on de bus
Drivers pan dem phone,
Yes, going full speed
And pan dem phone.
So now we a wonder if this is a blunder,
Technology causing we to go asunder.
Husband and wife have little time for each other,
Just because dem pan dem phone.

So where's your real attention
When you pan you phone?
Cause now dem a chase pokeman
Pan dem phone.
Is police paying attention
To all de lawless action?
There is just too much distraction
When dem pan dem phone.

A Passion

If you have a passion for something
Then you'll work diligently to excel at it.
Never mind the challenges you meet
And you may want to quit.
You'll pursue the journey,
Sometimes quickly, sometimes slowly,
And sometimes you may not have the urge at all.
Along the way you'll meet others
Who have similar interests.
You'll learn from them
That they're trudging the road, just like you.
A spark has been lit, and you move on again
With an enthusiasm you cannot explain.
So follow your passion and never give up,
You'll succeed where others have failed.

Limericks

Limericks

My dear Grandma whose name was Chrish,
She loved to cook corn meal and fish.
In the meal was the ochro
With one sweet potato,
It was a treat to savour this dish.

Officers are often late
And make the customers irate.
They don't apologise
Which might be very wise,
To change a bad situation to a positive state.

Walk slowly on the road when it is wet.
Then to your destination you will safely get.
Never cross swift flowing ghauts or rivers,
As these may give you the shivers
And to your safety they may be a threat.

Tom Cat whispered to his wife, Tabby Cat,
"I see a mouse but she's not very fat.
"She looks very old," said Tabby
Her little ones look shabby
Invite them to share the space on our mat.

Traveling can be exciting
When things are going to ones liking.
If there is a delay
Some get mad and say
Expletives that are just biting.

Who will count our numbers then?
Let us try from one to ten.
One, two, three, four and five,
Then onward strive
With six, seven, eight, nine, ten.

A monkey peeped around and thought,
These folks believe I'm really smart.
I reap what is sown,
Where ever it is grown,
And I certainly won't be caught.

Love is difficult to measure
If only few find it a treasure
It has so many forms
Which may exceed the norms.
In the end it should give much pleasure.

Often one has to compromise
So that progress can be made with an exercise
Get rid of negativity
In a worthwhile activity
Above the melee one has to rise.

The ferry sails across the sea
Some passengers are full of glee.
Some are serious,
Others appear nervous,
On the voyage for a spree.

Birds and bees fly all around,
Ants and snails crawl on the ground.
. Bats find it a delight
To fly only at night
While crickets chirp with a piercing sound.

One educator was standing up,
Couldn't understand the idea and seemed thunderstruck
In came Lady Powell
In her hand was a towel
And demonstrated the concept. What luck!

Kindly give our friend a call,
She broke her toe in a monstrous fall.
It may sound absurd,
She couldn't fly like a bird
To break the fall when she hit the wall.

Nature's Voice

Summer Therapy

The silver sand tickles my bare feet
As egrets are gliding by.
The greenery of nature sits admiring
As the children swim and float
In the bay.
Each wave caresses the body,
The breeze gently rocks a boat.
As the heat of the sun beats down,
I smile, as my toes sink in the sand;
Enjoying the summer therapy.

Bush Tea

My nostrils are tickled with the fragrance of the mint bush,
Some leaves are picked
To make bush tea.
As they are plunged into hot water, a delectable aroma exudes
which envelopes the kitchen
Magnetizing all the children.
The delicious bush tea is consumed by all
After adding a trifle of sugar.
Yet they would always admit,
It's the aroma that does the trick.

Nature Awoke

The thirsty land cried out,
My grass has gone so brown!
The animals seem to be grazing the dirt,
Asking, "When will it rain again?"

The leaves on the plants are wilting,
The hills and vales are bare.
Oh, how they mourn!
The heat is simply dehydrating human beings.

And suddenly, a deluge of rain,
The earth began to sing a green song.
And Mother Nature became awake it seemed,
When the bird choir started to sing.

Sunrise on Nevis Peak

Central she sits with silent lips
While gently sloping to her hips.
Admiring the entire land
She looks so humble yet so grand.
Enriched with morning's fragrant hue,
Poised like a monarch dressed in blue,
Our Queen of the Caribbean's mountain stands.

Ascending from the east, the sun
Creeps slowly o'er this dew-laden land.
Our blue dressed sovereign now gets set
To accept some heat and give off sweat.
Nature in all its beauty glows
In green and blue as sunrise shows
The glistening grass so wet.

The Bailey Trail

The Bailey Trail was an experience,
From start to finish it was quite intense.
With twenty three hikers on the trail
At eleven ten, didn't notice the oncoming gale.

The vote was on for the long or short trail,
Majority won, it was the long trail.
Our guide said it was a mile and three quarters,
We were soon to find out as she directed the charter.

A river with muddy water was roaring along
Yet none of us listened to her angry song.
Admiring heliconias, anthuriums and epiphytes
We trudged along in the dimming daylight.

Soon after the rain began to fall,
This should have been our retreat call.
So enthusiastic we were to see the parrots,
We plodded in single file as one unit.

Halfway on the trail everyone was soaked,
Having not even one raincoat.
By the time we reached the shelter of the huge old trees,
Admiring their broad roots didn't give us much ease.

Each hiker had to be very careful,
A slide could cause a perilous spill.
The comfort of having one mobile phone,
Gave us the advantage to call back home.

Sister said it was raining cats and dogs in town.
Another said her area also looked brown.
Lo and behold we had another river to cross,
This certainly would test who was the boss.

Our leaders tested the depth of the waters,
It was too deep and so we withdrew further.
Turning back, we examined the crossing,
While the furious waters were madly churning.

Each of us gave a sigh of relief
When the crossing was over, though it was very brief.
Next we witnessed a landslide reminding us it was time to go home
From our daring adventure, in this rainy zone.

One more bridge to cross and the trip was over,
The soiled shoes and clothes told a remarkable story.
Passports, tickets and money got wet.
What would Immigration think of these documents yet?

All said and done we gave thanks to the Almighty,
For helping us on this challenging journey.
The expedition was over we were on our way home,
Bailey Trail would be remembered for many days to come.

Welcome To Our Graduation

Graduation is a special occasion,
When students are honoured for their diligence.
It's a time when parents are excited
and the bond with our community is reignited.
However, we must never forget, the stress, the tears, the toil, the sweat,
That have been exerted at the primary level for seven long years.
Success just did not take place when Tests of Standards came,
It took years of commitment and dedication to show these gains.
For your presence on this Graduation Day,
Our Primary school warmly welcomes you, I say.

Moving On

Today, we're moving on and up,
And you are here to share with us.
We have to try and learn much more,
For education has great things in store.

We had to work hard here in school,
Teacher didn't allow us to play the fool.
Many thanks to our teachers we say
For the help they have given us all the way.

Learning has been fun each day
As we learned to interact, sing and play.
We are moving on to greater heights,
Where we will see some brighter lights.

Graduation, Harvest, Extravaganza

Graduation

It is our primary school's graduation,
And now it's time for our celebration.
We welcome all to this special occasion,
Sit back, relax, it's an academic function.

After working so hard for seven years,
Secondary school is now looming and there is no fear.
Parents have supported with encouragement,
Teachers have done their best with the syllabi content.

The future seems bright,
The best of our education is yet insight,
Welcome aboard as we take our flight!

Welcome - Harvest

Welcome to our Harvest Cantata
As we celebrate here at Combermere.
We are honoured to share this day with you,
As we sing and recite to you.
We hope that God would touch your life
As we worship side by side.
We hope you'll be blessed when you leave this place,
And you'll never forget "Harvest Cantata" here at Combermere.

Harvest Time

Harvest is a prosperous time,
When we give thanks to God.
For providing daily bread,
And drinks that we enjoy.

Our sweet potatoes are so tasty!
We thank you Lord for food --
Pumpkin, peas, tomatoes and peppers,
We thank you Lord for them all.

A Harvest

A harvest of pumpkins
A harvest of grain.
A harvest of bounty
And cool summer rain.

A harvest of souls
A harvest of love.
A harvest of mercy,
From our Father above.

Welcome Aboard

"Great is the Lord, and greatly to be praised!"
This is your flight attendant, Nijaunte David, welcoming you aboard
Flight Combermere Methodist Church Extravaganza Programme.
In command of the aircraft is our Lord Jesus Christ.
He will be ably assisted by First Officer, Captain Manners.
We are quite happy that you have decided to fly with us tonight.
We will be flying at an altitude you will always remember.
During the flight, you will be entertained by our guest artistes,
So kindly ensure that your seat belts are fastened as we prepare for
departure.
Ladies and gentlemen, boys and girls, please sit back, relax and enjoy
the flight.
Again I say, "Welcome aboard flight Combermere Methodist Church
Extravaganza Programme."

Our Extravaganza

Yes, the Extravaganza is over for certain,
We have just brought down the curtain.
Thanks for solos, duets and group songs
Through jazz, Country and Western and our little steel pan man,
Kenyon.

We glorified God in our celebration,
Which is truly needed in our small nation.
To Rev. Manners, thanks for being our facilitator;
Your message while chairing our programme couldn't have been
greater.

To our gracious audience, thanks for your presence,
Youth and older ones, we praised God with reverence.
Musicians all, thanks for your input,
That certainly flavoured the Extravaganza soup.

Displaying such natural talent here at Combermere,
Our Extravaganza says goodbye and thanks for being here.

Secular

The Investment

Clearly you're stepping on the road called success
By the Almighty you sure have been blessed.
A feeling of joy in your heart will arise
When, with ecstasy, you view this grand prize.
Each day just thank God for health and strength
Every moment he'll supply your needs at length.
Your investment has paid dividends
Which can take you to remarkable ends.

Investment Opportunity

To make more money one must invest,
Put all ones ideas to the test.
Put away the train track mentality
And use the helicopter idea with tenacity.

Don't worry about those who say you want to get rich,
Then worry from 'womb to tomb' with all kinds of itch.
Look around, see how you can improve on someone's idea,
Call a spade a spade and invest if you really care.

Focus on the big target, you can't go wrong.
Be passionate about it, you got to stick to it,
Like when you're in love when it's strong.
Share your ideas, look for an opportunity,
Then use the Joe Jeffers mentality and consultancy.
Take a few dollars and let's put them all together,
To start an investment opportunity.

Sorrel

Sorrel so red
Red like jasper.
Jasper, well polished
Polished ornaments and jewelry
Jewelry on my fingers
Fingers which are numb.
Numb and disfigured
Disfigured by years of hard work.

Paupers

So many days hunger was endured for you,
Because you were loved and that is true.
It was ensured care was taken of you,
And you were taught to do what is honest and true.

Imagine, you have a dwelling to live in,
Living like a queen or a king.
Is there a word of gratitude you have to share?
Yet you were taught to be honest and fair.

Education for you was free every day,
Church you attended each Lord's day.
Now that you have become adults
It seems you have joined the "lack of respect" cult.

Some attitudes thrive on the negative side,
By no law and order you want to abide.
Riches are scarce, that is very true,
Because parents have become paupers just for you!

Reflections, reflections, oh yes, we reflect
From one thing to another and this is direct.
Lord, help us to take what you have to offer,
Because for children's sake, some parents have become paupers.

Young Men

Fear and hatred
Hatred that causes crime
Crime that is killing
Killing our young men.

Men who are precious
Precious, youthful and strong
Strong to direct their children
Children who need guidance and wisdom.

Wisdom for a future
Future which could be bright
Bright and shining
Shining like stars in the sky.

Sky has no limit
Limit men's lives have now
Now that some bullets
Bullets have ended their lives senselessly.

Senselessly they have gone
Gone too soon
Soon with only mother to care
Care for their cherished offsprings.

Off springs who are angry
Angry with everyone
Everyone is concerned
Concerned for the lives of young men.

My Grandfather

My Grandfather's name was Dandy,
And people, my Dear Pops was handy.
He claimed that men should never be lazy
Or that alone might turn them crazy.
While walking home from church one Sunday,
Across the road scampered a furry animal.
"A mongoose! A mongoose!" Someone screamed,
And Grandpa in his stammering voice suddenly beamed.
"How come you say it is a "Mangoose?
Can't it be a 'womangoose'?"

Well friends, my sister visited from England
And drove straight to the home of our grandfather.
In his yard was Grandpa's brown little kitten.
Well, that is where we realized trouble was written.
When my excited sister questioned, "Grand Dad, what's the name
of your cat?
And he simply said, "Ye name cat – and dat is dat!"

The English lady seemed to think our elder a fool,
So she repeated the question like a teacher in school.
No Grand Dad, I mean, my name is Keevon
So could the name of your cat be possibly Beevon?
And Grandpa replied as calm as day,
"A say ye name cat, anyway."

Well, that might not have been bad enough.
The girl started to tell Grandpa some English stuff.
She told our grandpa, at home there is a Bullring
And that is where she does her weekend shopping.
Grandpa replied, "Girl, is so much beef you really buy?
Well those cattle paddock must be as wide as the sky".
"No Grandpa," she smiled "That is our shopping mall."
Grandpa declared, "Not even if grapes grow as big as pumpkins
I wouldn't believe that at all.

Immigration Toll

You left us here and went to yonder land,
To seek a better way of life so it was said.
Thanks to the loving, caring side of grandmother,
Who took time to aid my development with my brother.
Communication was mostly by way of postage letter then,
Your handwriting is well-known up to this day.
But how I wish I knew you more today, I regret to say
It is not so, because immigration took an awful toll.

My eyes were beaming when the postman came,
Though mails had little money all the same.
Yet, as a child, this was a dream come true.
A letter from my Mom was always due.
This connection was the thread I held on to,
As I also asked many questions too.
Besieged by many thoughts both night and day,
When immigration took my Mom away.

At Bailey Bush, those mangoes were so sweet
At times, they were the only fruits I craved to eat.
Early mornings soon after I awoke from sleep,
First chore was to the pasture we took the sheep,
Then up a mango branch I'd climb with such agility,
Onlookers were amazed by my agile ability.
Happy days I now recall with Mama's mould,
When immigration held my parents for a toll.

Siblings, I was told about for sure,
Their names from memory I could procure.
All dates of births and many other things,
But these things move with fleeting wings.
A photo now and then I held as treasure,
And closely examined them for my own pleasure.
But these couldn't replace the loss I felt within,
When immigration took its terrible toll.

On Mother's wedding day, surely I was absent.
Probably couldn't afford for us to be present.
To make things even worse, more like a curse,
The wedding cake was sent to Grandpa in a purse.
I hoped in vain to get a little taste,
But maybe Grandpa thought 'twould be a waste.
Absent again was that little girl,
When immigration took another toll.

Eager to make the link, I booked a flight,
My mind excited glowed like shining light.
Wrote a letter to say I'll pay a visit,
A reply returned that up to now I can't emit.
Disappointment reigned o'er my jaded face,
I wondered how on earth this could take place.
My wicket was knocked down and sure clean bowled
As once again old immigration took its toll.

Primary, High School, College and University
Have all escaped the notice, just a pity.
No success have you witnessed here with me.
How can such things escape ones family?
Given a two year invitation in advance,
To attend my graduation just by chance.
But now my brother's illness took priority
As immigration dealt another blow to me.

In all our years, there was a four week visit,
'Twas all we got to try to form a knit.
But certain things in life don't work like magic,
And this is one of life's best kept secret.
Big brother came and cried just like a babe,
The aching void I guess just could not fade.
I believe we saw his hurt that day unfold,
But then, immigration had taken its toll.

At age twelve, Dad returned from England in his velvet cap,
For an impolite answer to Mama, from him I got a slap.
But Oh! That was a mistake which he made,
Mama launched on him in an awful tirade.
I could only just imagine how he felt
With this blow to him that was severely dealt.
Sadly, only she was to discipline his only girl,
Which indicated how immigration had taken its toll.

Just can't be ungrateful to my Dear Old Grand,
A stalwart, she's the best known in my stand.
For education she always gave a shout,
And gave to me an opportunity, anywhere about.
Encouragement was in abundance all the way;
She always had high hopes for me each day.
Had it not been for this generous, gracious girl,
Immigration might have had a much worse toll.

No matter what happens in this life to me,
Each member of my family will see.
My dear Old Mama has a special place,
As for her throughout life I'll make a case.
And forever, in this life before I go
I'll always be proud to let the whole world know
Her charming smile, her vigilance, her care,
Stood like a beacon, when immigration took its toll.

A Man of Integrity

A man of integrity courage and pride
Was born in Nevis on the Windward side.
His decision was made to join the military,
Where he gained knowledge and experience from the police
constabulary.

His fearlessness and loyalty helped him overcome obstacles;
In the armed force, he reached great pinnacles.
Days and nights in the field guarding us from contraband,
He has given yeoman's service to this land.

Guns missing! Who was present on duty?
Something seemed mysterious. Did other officers see?
Were weapons and ammunition left unguarded carelessly?
Something in this whole affair is puzzling to me.

Years of honourable service to our Federation
Has come to an indefinite suspension! What is this?
An honest report? A set up? A dishonourable discharge?
Or is the real culprit in the country still at large?

This is your moment to reminisce my brother,
Keep calm and still be courteous, continue to be wise as ever.
Keep up your dignity and hold your head high.
You will understand it better by and by.

Kevonique

Kind, loving and she is Keen
Endearing and sometimes to learn she is Eager
Verbose and full of Vitality
Observant and most times Occupied
Noteworthy and Noisy
Individual with immediate Imagery
Questioning and Quick
Understanding and Unshrinking
Enthusiastic and Evasive

Eviction or Promotion

One said, I believe that teachers should be transferred as all other officers do.
That was alright, if it was done with respect, dignity and common courtesy
too.
Knowing the years of our contribution to education, that did not matter at all
Whether the institution did well; one did not care if there was a vendetta to call.

At some point in time, each institution had excellent results, top student I daresay.
Then, during graduation the officials would beam and give a pat on the shoulder that day.
With performance and perspiration along the way, sometimes going beyond duty's call,
Some didn't care about that, just tread carefully or you fall.

Well, sometimes members undermine their own institution.
No matter how much good some officers do, still a single fault is like a great abomination.
If we continue this way to try and kill our own and then say others are taking over,
We've got to cover our backs with wisdom, be professional and try and pull our system back.

A decent assignment is different to a so called 'eviction promotion'.
Education must never be tampered as we must have officers who are
performing.
As leaders we have to work to educate our nation's children,
Having goals set and the future with a vision.

The Villain

It was done wrongly from the start
Behaving as if she had mastered fine art.
Just flared up and without even thinking
About the bitter cup from which she was drinking.

The eyes ablaze, the nostrils flared,
Seemed as if lightning struck on the head.
To change the clothing, home I'll go
And start a great comedian show.

Police involved, problem not solved
And parents got real mad.
Come on now teacher, what do you preach?
Communication channels all gone bad.

Leader now got into the fray,
Had to learn of the melodramatic melee.
To solve the problem, called in police, parents and teacher
To bring things back in order.

What Christmas Means

The Christmas story in the Bible was foretold
By Isaiah, the prophet of old.
Christmas must truly be in our hearts as we live from day to day,
Sharing and caring for each other, along life's way.

There were three wise men, who came from the East,
And shepherds abiding in the fields who didn't have a feast.
Mary gave birth to her baby in a stable so humble,
There was no hospital and she didn't grumble.

Today, our families are busy preparing,
Buying new clothes and shoes and extra food for dining.
The hams and the turkeys and the cakes we are baking,
Along with the sorrel that we will be drinking.

Each year we admire the glitz and glamour
Commercializing the Advent season from October to December.
Let's teach old and young about forgiveness this Christmas;
Having our souls saved from sin and being His witness.

But after the physical needs have been met,
There is still a lot more that we have to get.
We need some spiritual nourishment each day,
In order to survive Satan's attacks along the way.

Enjoying Christmas must help us to reflect
On our sins and the price Jesus paid for our debt.
That was his coming, now we are seeing signs of the end,
The signs abound that Christ is coming again.

Today, Christ calls for me and for you,
To accept Him in our hearts, everyone, not just a few.
He's pleading and calling from the realms on high,
He wants us to live with Him by and by.

Life's Battles

The Asian Tragedy

It was a disaster on an unprecedented scale
As survivors told horrific tales.
A tsunami struck in Asia on Sunday, twenty-sixth December,
Angry waves drowned thousands, destroyed homes and loved ones.

Villages were swept away
From the epicentre at Banda Aceh.
Along the coast of Sri Lanka,
Destruction was unimaginable in Sumatra.

Indonesia, India and Thailand needed help,
The Maldives, Andaman and Nicobar couldn't understand themselves.
Consternation, grief, weeping and wailing,
Traumatized and hungry; plus aftershocks, even more frightening.

The magnitude of this disaster needed international effort.
Heart-broken survivors needed food, shelter, water and comfort.
The rest of the world sent aid in vast proportions;
Donors recognized the need for mass coordination.

Danger of diseases was another problem,
Along with burial of the dead by those who were traumatized.
Never in recent history was there such a mammoth disaster,
Which came from the tectonic bed of the Indian Ocean destroyer.

In just a few minutes, the end came for hundreds of thousands,
As nature's fury unleashed, many scampered for higher ground.
History was made in the region forever,
By the December 2004 tsunami disaster.

Why? Oh Why?

A telephone call came in at two,
Which said he could not be found.
Where had he gone that Sunday morn?
'Twas the second time he walked away.

The surrounding grounds were combed,
The ghauts, the hills and dale
Across the springs and in the vale;
This certainly was strange.

The community became concerned
And joined to help the family,
And then so suddenly,
One sibling walked into the house.

There was absolute distress,
His face seemed dazed and so listless,
Shock reigned upon his countenance,
Utter disbelief was on his resonance.

A sudden shriek, a wail!
Then came the heart wrenching, gloomy tale.

International Crises

Bombing in the city, July 7th what a morn!
In a few moments, fifty three lives were gone
Commotion, confusion, stress levels rising,
Creating fear in persons who were travelling.

G-8 Summit was taking place in Scotland,
One Prime Minister had to leave and rush home to his land.
Who would perform those notorious and cowardly acts?
Was the question asked by citizens under attack.

The Darfur crisis now slid onto the backburner,
Only to see the ghastly sight of famished children in Reager.
Heat waves struck in the United States and France,
Earthquakes in other countries drove people's minds into a trance.

Another bomb scare a fortnight later,
Angered law enforcement officers who were placed under pressure.
It was alleged that one by police was slaughtered.
It was said that one turned out to be a martyr.

On the edge of Africa there were more blows from more bombs,
One important tourist resort now lay in ruin.
Wondering if this was someone's bidding,
Behind which terrorists were hiding.

Hitting at the hearts of economies and destabilising lives.
Resilience must now raise it head. Freedom must not be deprived!
Around the globe there are so many wars,
Leaving grieving families with terrible scars.

Intoxicated By Music

Imposingly, he dealt some blows,
Upon the drum to rid his woes.
His body capered to and fro
As palms, in hurricane manoeuvre.
He seemed in his world all alone
This gave him joy we could discern.
A smile he gave with sheer delight
Upon his face all gleaming bright;
Intoxicated by music.

He leapt behind the drum and danced
Head over heels that boy would prance.
And then another somersault
Followed by a cantering waltz.
The horn blast now just made him slide
Like hikers on a mountain side.
One couldn't miss his carousing
As revellers did wine and sing;
Intoxicated by music.

And as the notes were slowing down,
He slumped on to the dusty ground.
Moaning, he looked so worn and dazed,
Seemed like his mind was in a haze.
His costume drenched with perspiration
Drew all the spectators' attention.
Wobbling, he now tried to stand
But lost his balance and grabbed my hand;
Intoxicated by music.

Precious Memories

Our day started as usual,
Everything seemed normal.
We had no idea that day would bring,
A change in life, with everything!

You said you did not feel so well,
How your body felt, I can't exactly tell.
To work, our several ways we went
Not expecting that serious incident.

A telephone call came to my work that sunny morn
To say your speech had been withdrawn.
I rushed home with such urgency,
Not knowing it was a fatal emergency.

Family and friends were called at that hour,
All rushed to the hospital's tower.
You did not respond to our mortal call,
We cried, we prayed, we tried our all.

Physicians here all tried their best,
Realized this was past earthly test.
Overseas help could do no more.
You were taken to the other shore.

Memories of you will linger on,
In deed, and word, and thought and song.
Your serving Christ sure made the difference
In that we'll always have confidence.

A rose was chosen in full bloom,
For the heavenly garden you had to groom.
Quietly, you slipped away.
Hope to meet you in heaven one day.

Hurricane Irma

Well, Hurricane Irma had some action,
That caused some Caribbean Islands mass destruction.
She came across the Atlantic Ocean in a rage,
And set her eye on Barbuda as her first stage.

As a Category Five Hurricane, meteorologists warned that things
looked grave.
Implored citizens and residents to prepare themselves to save,
Move from the coastline to higher ground,
Do not take any chances or later you may not be found.

Having unleashed its full fury on the tiny island of Barbuda,
The warrior churned towards St. Kitts and Nevis, Barbuda's neighbours.
She suddenly decided to change course and travel north-west,
Down to St. Martin Irma headed for its next conquest.

Anguilla got the full blast of this category five storm as well.
All essential services were down this must have been somewhat like
hell.
Gone was the hospital, schools destroyed, people became homeless
in minutes.
Irma was destructive and threw many into panic.

Heading over land people thought that Irma would slow down.
Not a bit, this angry beast decided she would wear the hurricane crown.
Tortola, St. John, Virgin Gorda and Anegada were minced like meat.
The Chief Minister had to call a State of Emergency from his
honourable seat.

Not tired as yet, Irma whipped St. Thomas with ease,
The count was now on for fatalities.
Rich and poor, big and small cowered with fear,
No matter who or what you were, Hurricane Irma didn't care.

Continuing on its path of mass destruction,
Puerto Rico and Cuba were now on for their interruption.
Their north eastern coasts failed to escape her wrath,
Irma was charging at anything in her path.

Monster Irma had the Turks and Caicos Island in sight.
Anxiety filled people's minds, things didn't look bright.
The Bahamas were now preparing for this brigadier,
As Florida had panic stricken people catapulting with fear.

Well social media now had a feast,
Showing damages and destruction, to say the least.
The English, French and Dutch aristocrats flew down;
The northern Caribbean was the center of attention for the colonial
crowns.

September 2017 will certainly be remembered
For the onslaught brought by Hurricane Irma's drama.
Time to look at global warming seriously,
We cannot afford to become climate refugees.

The Best is Yet to Come

Poor Larry seemed to be so confused,
When he had to relay the unbelieveable news.
According to the Boss, you won't give the Vote of Thanks,
Poor fellow, he almost went into a trance.

Wondering now if I'm a Nevisian
Or maybe a terrorist or Syrian.
How can we be so awful, then call on God's name
Maybe the Master is hanging His head in shame.

Quiet, my girl, the best is yet to come
Don't argue, don't fuss, let the course take its run.
Just fold your arms, look to God and pray.
You will see your eyes full, one day.

Little wonder it was said I shouldn't be seen on TV
The problem is, some people can't appreciate the talent they see
At the end of the day when we give an account
Some will say yes, she has been on the mount.

Nevis Welcomes You

The Girls Brigade in Nevis warmly welcomes you
To serve, to seek to follow Christ is our common view
To Nevis, he has led you, to spread His word around,
In Nevis then, the Girls Brigade, will stand on Christ's firm ground.

Amidst your busy schedules
Enjoy our island's serenity
Be immersed by a breath taking sunrise
Be embraced by our tranquillity.

As the Caribbean breezes caress your face,
Our Girls Brigade warmly welcomes you to this place.

Retirement

Never be afraid to retire
While there is good health and strength!
When you have served honestly
And given valuable service at length.
Think about the possibilities
Which will be new each day
Viewing life from another perspective.
Think about the many things
You've always wanted to do
And place them in your memory bank
Marked, "Aspirations New."
Think about a budget and how you'll spend your income
For a rainy day, you'll still have to save some.
Think about the service you'll keep doing for mankind,
And surely an enjoyable retirement you'll find.

Upon Retirement

To the many lives I would have touched,
I want to thank you so very much
For giving me that opportunity,
To express my poetic creativity.

Printed in the United States
By Bookmasters